KIDS FOR NATURE
Inspiring children to become caretakers of the world.

Hello, I'm SeedSpook

I call myself that as I like to do gardening, but not just at home. I also do it outdoors whenever I go for walks, and I always wear my hood up so nobody recognises me. That's right...I grow flowers and plant trees in barren places. Do you like nature and wildlife as much as me?

Nature has been around forever. Long before humans came along, and will be around long after we are gone. Even in deep space, nature is working hard mixing gases and heat and creating new things.

Here on our planet, Earth, it also works hard. Trees work especially hard giving out the oxygen we need to breath. Bees and other flower friendly insects pollinate the plants so we can have fruit and vegetables. Whales that filter-feed on plankton help cleanse the oceans and seas.

Nature and wildlife are so important, but people are so busy we often forget just how much. But did you know, even YOU can help take care of them? This book will show you how to become an expert carer of wildlife and nature, even if you are very young.

DEDICATION

To my late father, whom I did not have nearly
enough time with.

<u>PART 1</u>

HABITATS

A habitat is an area certain animals make there home. Did you know, if you have a garden you probably already have a few habitats? It's true.

Fences, walls, lawns and pebbles are also habitats. Take a look! On a fence you may see a spider living quite happily. On walls you can find tiny mites living on the stonework. Lawns have lots of bugs living in it. Pebbles are also good homes for beetles and bugs. It is important to be sensible when looking around habitats. Only show off's and idiots would disturb them and frighten wildlife.

But let's learn how to make some more habitats and attract more wildlife to our gardens. Maybe you can also make some in parks and woodland?

LOG PILES

Even something as easy as making a pile of sticks and logs is enough to draw much more wildlife into your garden. They are items we can find anywhere and when piled up neatly they make a very nice looking feature in your garden.

They also make a very wonderful home for spiders, beetles, bugs and other insects. Woodlice will enjoy them in particular. Better still, frogs and toads may crawl under and hide there throughout winter.

Who would have thought something so easy can be something important? You can even build them in parks, woods and by the seaside once you find enough wood.

ROCKERY

Rather in the same way a log pile gives homes and shelter to wildlife, a rockery will also do the same.

The stones keep in a lot of heat when the sun is shining, which is ideal for reptiles like this common lizard, who lives under the stones when it is cold, or sun bathes on them when it is hot.

Seeing reptiles is an especially rare sight. If you are lucky enough to see one please leave it, they do not make good pets, and they may even have a nest nearby. Be smart, look but don't touch and you will enjoy these lovely animals for a long time.

<u>WATER DISH</u>

There are no animals I can think of that do not need water. We need it as much as we need oxygen in the air. Without water we would not live for more than a few days as our bodies would dry out.

Adding a water dish to your garden can attract a lot of wildlife, becoming a mini cafe for birds and bugs alike. Many birds also like to swim in water dishes to clean and cool down, so be sure to check it several times a day and make sure it is clean.

Do not over fill the water dish. About a centimetre deep is perfect and will allow small creatures that may fall in a chance to escape.

TREES

Trees are homes to literally hundreds of species, including birds, bees and bats. They are also essential for life, giving us lots of oxygen while taking in polluted gases. They are our natural air conditioners.

Every large adult tree will produce enough oxygen for 10 people a year, but it takes four trees to take in the carbon just one person produces in a lifetime. They can also be a food source, giving us fruit and nuts.

If your garden isn't big enough for a large tree, consider some small fruit trees like my father in this photo. Even a conifer is plenty for a blackbird to nest in.

COMPOST HEAP

A compost heap is the heart of any garden. You can throw all of your green waste on it such as grass clippings, vegetable peelings, fallen leaves, even rabbit and chicken poo.

Sprinkle over a small layer of soil every few inches. The worms will set to work eating all the waste and turning it into fresh garden compost like magic. Keep it moist, but not too wet so ants do not try to nest in it. Gradually you will be left with nitrogen-rich compost for planting new things.

Be warned, as things break down the heap will warm up, and maybe even steam on cold mornings. If it is cold, turn it over and re-pile it to get things going again. Be careful of frogs or grass-snakes that may be sheltering inside.

<u>BUG HOTEL</u>

Another very important feature is a bug hotel. They provide great homes for solitary bees, ladybirds and caterpillars. As we humans chop down more and more woodland, these bugs need somewhere to live. Face your bug hotel south and about a meter off the ground.

The one in the photo was purchased at a shop, but you can also get a grown-up to make you one for free by finding a good thick log and drilling holes 5mm-12mm across and four to five inches deep. Drill them slightly tilted upwards so rain does not flood the holes.

If they have a cordless drill, maybe you could take them to the woods or beach to find logs to drill. Please do not drill into trees though, this can make them diseased and die.

PART 2

SEEDBALLS

In the early 1900s live a woman named Ellen Ann Willmott. She loved gardening, and had a habit of visiting other gardeners and dropping seeds of the flower Eryngium Giganteum. It is an act known today as seed-bombing. She became so fond of this plant it was eventually name after her - Miss Willmott's Ghost.

It is one of my favourite plants too, looking striking and packed with nectar. Ellen may be the very reason I am writing this book today as I like to seed-bomb too. Some use the method Ellen used, just sprinkling the seeds. Another method is seedballing, and I will now teach you how to make seedballs which you can drop anywhere you think they might grow and look nice. This is a wonderful way to grow things if you do not have a garden.

You will need:

<u>Red Potters Clay</u>
You can usually buy this ready made in packets, or as a powder to mix with water.

<u>Compost</u>
All purpose compost to aid plant growth.

<u>Seeds</u>
Some love bee friendly meadow flower seeds will be great but you can choose others, even fruit and veg, or tree seeds for big areas.

<u>Water</u>
To help mix it all together. Now follow the following steps.

Get yourself a lovely big mixing bowl and mix one handful of potters clay to two handfuls of compost. Once you are finished it should look a lovely even colour and no lumps. If it feels to dry, add just a tiny bit of water.

Roll the mix into little balls about 2cm across. Poke a small hole into it with your fingertip. Not too far, about half a centimetre to a centimetre is fine.

Gently drop some seeds into the hole. The ones in this picture are Rowan tree berries.

Now seal the hole up and roll back into a ball. Hey presto, you have a seedball. Repeat the process until you have finished and leave them to dry out in a warm area.

You can now go out and deploy these in dull looking areas. The clay will keep the seed safe as it grows, and the compost will nourish it. Seedballing is a modern term, but is a practise that is centuries old, and used today in professional reforestation projects around the world.

PART 3

WONDERFUL ANIMALS

Every animal has a purpose in life. In nature there are some more helpful than others. The bee is incredibly important. It not only pollinates our fruit and vegetable plants, it makes lovely sweet honey. Did you know, honey is one of the only foods that never goes bad?

This photo by Jamie Fry, shows a bee covered in pollen dust. It will now fly to another plant where these bits will fall off and pollinate it, making it fruit. We must protect bees at all costs. They will only sting if you try to touch them aggressively. Like all natures animals, they do not need touching as they are not pets.

LADYBIRDS

There are many different species of ladybirds, although we mainly think of the ones which are red with black spots. These are a wonderful friend to have in the garden as they will eat pests like greenfly.

They will hibernate in confined areas in
the cold months, all huddled together.
Having a pile of leaves in the garden is a
great home for them. Keep the leaves in a
wire mesh cage to stop them blowing
away in the wind.

BATS

Bats are becoming so increasingly rare
now like a lot of wild animals. This bat
didn't have a proper home. I found it
asleep on a wall under a bridge, and took

a photo quickly before leaving it alone. Bats will help keep the population of moths down. You can buy specially made bat boxes to hang up near your roof, and larger trees provide good homes for them too. By now I hope you are beginning to see why it is so important we take every chance to help nature where we can.

<u>SLOW WORM</u>

At first glance you would think a slow worm is a tiny snake but it is really a lizard that has evolved without legs. It's duties in the garden involve controlling fly, bugs and spider populations and it likes plenty of long undisturbed grassy areas and a rockery. You should never try to pick one up as their tails can detach. This is a defence known as autotomy, which helps them escape predators.

HEDGEHOGS

Sadly many of us only see hedgehogs when it is too late. They usually get killed trying to cross the networks of roads we use on a daily basis. Another example of a wild animal that can benefit from some kindness is we provide it a shelter.

In return, they will help keep and slug problems you may have under control, and who knows, you may be lucky

enough to have an entire family of them
in your back garden.

Horatio here, belongs to hedgehog expert,
Justina Ford-Brown, who took this photo.

  You can buy hedgehog homes ready
made but they are also rather easy to
make if you have the correct materials.
The plan view in this diagram shows just
how basic it is. I followed it using bricks,

then a wooden roof covered in lots of wooden pieces.

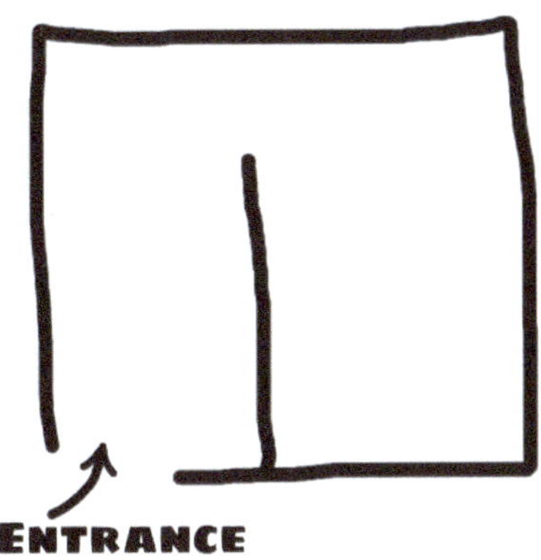

And here it is finished, about a week later we was blessed with a visitor.

PART 4

PLANTS

I shall now list a few extremely good plants, starting with stinging nettles. Not many of us like these as brushing against them is very painful. But did you know, stinging nettles are important to over 30 different species of butterfly?

It's true! They are more good than they are bad so if you can save a small patch of nettles in your garden where nobody

really goes, you'll be doing a great job for
nature.

<u>FRATILLERY</u>

Early flowering plants such as this
Snakeshead Fratillery will keep early bees
just waking up from hibernation fed.

Maybe you could also add daffodils and crocus too for early springtime colour.

AGASTACHE

Of all the easiest plants to grow this must be one of the easiest and highest in nectar. It looks like a stinging nettle but then a tall purple flower rises from it attracted bees, hoverflies and butterflies alike. If you squish an agastache leaf in your fingers, the oils have a lovely aniseed scent. It self-seeds every year, so be careful to grow it in a contained area otherwise it will become a bit intrusive.

LAVENDER

Everybody knows the smell of lavender, and in the height of Summer you can see bees feeding in droves upon the flowers. It's scent is used largely in air fresheners and perfumes, but the oils can also be refined and used to flavour cakes.

A lot of people find the scent of lavender

overpowering, and if you are one of those people then fear not. Try growing borage instead. It is really easy from seed.

SEA HOLLY

Sea Holly is another extremely high nectar plant which all the pollinators will love. They grow quite tall and have electric-blue flowers that look like stars.

FINAL MESSAGE

I hope you have enjoyed reading my little book, and you go out there and make some habitats or do some seedballing. Just the tiniest bit of effort from people can make a huge difference.

You don't have to be clever or rich to help change the world, you just need to be sensible and responsible. Maybe one day I will be walking along and enjoying things you have grown or built for wildlife. Keep sensible and safe, SeedSpook x